ISBN-13: 978-0-692-11648-7

DEDICATION

This book is dedicated to YOU. You have been blessed with a unique gift and must live your life with passion, desire and happiness. There is no other person in the world like you. Nobody else will ever think, speak or see things the way you do. Always follow your instincts and make sure to live your life with joy. Find positivity in everything you do and make sure to always see the best in life

Pay Attention: Things you need to know if you want to *BE HAPPIER AT WORK*

Dr. Eric Roberts

Inv. Lorena Mendez

Seek to understand
before being
understood

CONTENTS

ACKNOWLEDGMENTS

We thank God for providing us with the ups and downs in life that have given us the opportunities to become better. Each experience is a gift that has helped us grow.

ALWAYS BE PROFESSIONAL

The way you present yourself to the world is an important aspect of your success. Unfortunately, many people do not recognize if their behavior is professional. It is important to analyze yourself and understand you may have to change the way you behave to ensure you are presenting yourself in a manner that allows others to see you as a positive representative of the organization. When you work for an organization, you represent it. Do not make a habit of displaying or delivering your own personal beliefs. You must limit sharing your personal beliefs to your own time.

When you are at work, the time belongs to the organization, not you. Acting professionally is ensuring you are a person the organizational leaders are proud of and that they are not ashamed of acknowledging your employment. At times, you may have to be a different person at work than you are at home; however, this does not mean going against your personal values and beliefs. You must always be respectful and not let your personal beliefs impede the performance of your daily tasks and goals. Whether or not you like a person at work should not dictate the way you treat him or her. ***Take the high road and be the mature adult***. Remember, you represent the organization. Always ask yourself, "If I owned a company, am I behaving the way I would want my employees to behave?" If the answer is no, then you need to make some changes and view things differently.

PROFESSIONALISM IS NOT A LABEL YOU GIVE YOURSELF, IT IS A DESCRIPTION YOU HOPE OTHERS WILL APPLY TO YOU

DAVID MAISTER

CONTROL YOUR EMOTIONS

The ability to control your emotions can be challenging. ***It is important to learn how to manage your feelings***. Everybody has a set of core values and beliefs. Often times, core values and beliefs cause people to become emotional. If anyone violates the values that others believe in passionately, often strong feelings are involved. If you are going to be successful, you must not be driven by emotions. Do not let your values and principles cause you to behave in a manner that is unprofessional.

There will be times when someone says something that you either do not agree with, or feel about very strongly. Before you decide to respond or act against them, be mindful of your surroundings and the consequences of your actions. Once you decide to act based on emotion, there will always be aspects of the situations that are missed. Your emotions will allow you to see things one way and miss some other perspectives. If you have to, walk away from the situation before deciding to respond.

DO NOT LET YOUR EMOTIONS DISTRACT YOU FROM DOING WHAT NEEDS TO BE DONE. CONTROL YOUR EMOTIONS OR YOUR EMOTIONS WILL CONTROL YOU

UNKNOWN

BE CONSISTENT

It is impossible to be successful without the element of consistency. You work many hours in a day and have goals. You must find the daily actions and routine that creates the desired results. Once you find the actions and routines, continue to follow them regularly to create the consistent behavior necessary for long-term results.

All employers like reliable employees. To be a stand-out employee, you must show consistency, which means being on time consistently, following through with what you said you would do consistently, and behaving in a way that people trust you will make the best decision consistently for the organization. *Consistent behavior builds trust*. Once you have the trust of your employer, you increase your chances of obtaining an opportunity for growth within the organization.

SUCCESS IS NOT ALWAYS
ABOUT GREATNESS. IT
IS ABOUT CONSISTENCY.
CONSISTENT HARD WORK
LEADS TO SUCCESS.
GREATNESS WILL COME

DWAYNE JOHNSON

CREATE A VISION

Without vision, you are going nowhere. *You must have an idea of where you want to go to be happy and successful.* When you are working towards something, it allows you to maintain the focus necessary to achieve satisfaction. What are you trying to accomplish by working at this job? Where do you see yourself in the next 1 to 2 years? These questions are not easy to answer, but you need to begin thinking about them to obtain peace. You will be frustrated and annoyed if you are unable to see yourself achieving some type of professional progress.

Having an idea of how you could possibly achieve professional growth creates a sense of direction and purpose. If you are not moving in a specific direction, it is very hard to be satisfied with your daily routine. Working a job just to pay the bills is not a sufficient vision. It is critical for your sanity to find purpose at work and take actions that will lead to future opportunities that excite you.

A MAN WITHOUT A VISION FOR HIS FUTURE ALWAYS RETURNS TO HIS PAST

UNKNOWN

BE HUMBLE

There must always be a sense of value and appreciation for whatever you do to keep you grounded. It is okay to be happy with what you have, but desire more growth; it is a delicate balance that most people get wrong. Being humble does not mean you have to settle or be satisfied. ***Seek to obtain more knowledge and understanding and never put others down for your own benefit***.

Do not let your pride get in the way of future opportunities. Too often, people let their values and principles ruin their chances of making progress. As long as you are not being disrespected or taken advantage of, you will need to be humble and accept situations. There will be times when people make mistakes that will have a negative impact on you. First, do not take it personally. Secondly, understand that everyone makes mistakes. Although it is not fair, it is reality. Humble yourself and do not act as though you will or can never make the same mistake or worse, which is where humility needs to be applied. Remember, if it was not intentional, humble yourself and move on. This should not stop you from moving forward.

believe you may not achieve the desired outcome. Regardless, commit to the necessary actions to get to the end.

COMMITMENT LEADS TO ACTION.
ACTION BRINGS YOU CLOSER TO YOUR DREAM

MARCIA WIEDER

HAVE GOOD INTENTIONS

Although we all know what is right and what is wrong, the truth is that being 100% ethical can be challenging. Mistakes will be made. People have a natural habit of protecting themselves, while truly not wanting to hurt others. The protective habit forces most people to be untruthful, and creates a constant battle between the truth and what people want others to believe. It is important to do your best and have good intentions. If you make a mistake and do something unethical, analyze the situation and determine the reason for your actions. Do your best not to make the unethical behavior a habit. It would be unrealistic to believe you will never say the wrong thing or do something you knew was wrong. ***Always work on improving yourself and learn from your actions so you will stay on a path of being the most ethical and honest version of yourself.***

Do not judge others if they are unethical. As previously mentioned, people want to protect themselves. If they are lying, cheating, or stealing, they have already justified their actions and know the consequences. Do your best not to get involved, and avoid making the person feel as if you are better. Seek within yourself to understand why the person's behavior is unethical. This will allow you to learn and possess a better understanding of human behavior as you continue to grow in life.

YOU ARE WHAT YOU DO, NOT WHAT YOU SAY YOU WILL DO

UNKNOWN

BE TRUSTWORTHY

Before evaluating your level of trust in other people, you must assess yourself first. Can you be trusted? The answer could solve many problems you may have with being unhappy at work. People know what people can be trusted and who cannot be trusted. To keep it simple, make sure you keep your word and do not gossip about other people. When you gossip about individuals' professional or personal lives, it indicates you may do the same to people with whom you are speaking, thus separating the people who can and cannot be trusted.

Some people in life will never trust anyone. Do not take it personally. Just because you may be a trustworthy person does not mean everyone will treat you the same way. This often occurs in the workplace. Many people work to survive and are very careful not to trust anyone. They distrust because they feel someone may reveal what they really think about other people and the organization. Some may gossip simply to see what you think and use it to their advantage. So, you do not have to be concerned, *keep things simple and*

only say positive things about everyone and the organization. As the old saying goes, "If you don't have anything positive to say, don't say anything at all".

BEING TRUSTWORTHY REQUIRES: DOING THE RIGHT THING AND DOING THINGS RIGHT

DON PEPPERS

DO NOT TAKE THINGS PERSONALLY

Most decisions are made to preserve the organization and preserve the individuals who made the decisions. If you ever find yourself in a situation where you feel someone has made a decision specifically directed toward you, think twice and ask yourself, "What is the individual gaining from taking that particular action or saying those words." Often, organizational leaders do not think of individuals when they make decisions. Their motive is money and they want to ensure that the daily actions of the employees are going to increase chances of profits. Few people wake up in the morning and say they are going to make every effort to make a certain person's life miserable.

Often times, it is a momentary decision by someone to attack or demean another person, which is done typically to make the individual feel better about self. If you are constantly around someone who exhibits this behavior, you must be proactive and take action so it does not continue. If someone is consistently directing negative comments and attention towards you, address it in private, so it does not continue to occur. If the actions are not consistent, do not give the action much attention. Too many people believe decisions and comments are about them and worry too much about what others think. This is a distraction and will limit your ability to be creative. *The more time you spend worrying about how people feel about you, the less time you will have to accomplish your goals.*

WHAT OTHER PEOPLE THINK ABOUT YOU IS NONE OF YOUR BUSINESS

UNKNOWN

COMMUNICATE WITH OTHERS

The most valuable asset a person possesses is the ability to communicate. The only way to be an effective communicator is to be clear and direct in what you are saying. Many people hesitate to say what they really mean. You must be confident in what you are saying, and be open to listening to what the other person is saying. Most people do not listen. People spend too much time trying to think of what they want to say to get their point across, instead of just listening. ***The ability to listen is the most important aspect of effective communication.*** You will understand more of what the person is communicating and meaning if you take time to listen.

Translating a conversation is another component of being an effective communicator. If you listen and watch body language, you will have a better understanding of the conversation. Does the person want you to read between the lines? If what the other person is saying to you does not make sense, trust your instincts and realize there is more to the conversation than what is being said. Do not take the communication personally. People are only protecting themselves. Simple awareness of knowing that there is more to the conversation is enough to allow you to communicate better. Communication is more than speaking with another individual. Understanding body language, tone, feelings, and the unspoken meanings is crucial in effective communication.

THE MOST IMPORTANT THING IN COMMUNICATION IS HEARING WHAT ISN'T BEING SAID

SHANNON ALDER

ADAPT TO THE SITUATION

You must have the ability to adapt to many different situations. Throughout life, you will find yourself in various types of uncomfortable situations. Do not shy away from such moments. *Learn to be comfortable with being uncomfortable*. Often, when you are uncomfortable, you want to avoid being in the moment. Being nervous and scared is okay as long as you do not let it stop you from moving forward. Following this model will allow you to be more comfortable in different types of circumstances. As long as you maintain your professionalism and respect for others, you must learn how to deal with different situations, which will only enhance your skill sets and teach you how to handle different types of situations readily.

YOU MUST ADAPT TO
YOUR SURROUNDINGS
WITHOUT LOSING
YOURSELF IN THE
PROCESS

INV. MENDEZ

BE WILLING TO SACRIFICE

Employers are always looking for individuals who are willing to make a sacrifice for the betterment of the organization. Sacrifice is often displayed in the form of time. Avoid saying no quickly if you are asked to stay late, take on additional responsibilities, or work during your day off. Although it should not occur often, *the sacrifice of your willingness to accept the requests will help you in the long run.* Organizational leaders will always see these types of sacrifices as a great quality in an employee and the quality often leads to more opportunities in the organization. It is common for managers to make such sacrifices. As you begin to accept more responsibility in your work life, it will be common practice. Be okay with sacrificing a little personal time, but make sure to read the section on work-life balance.

SACRIFICE TODAY TO OBTAIN A BETTER TOMORROW

UNKNOWN

PAY ATTENTION TO OFFICE POLITICS

What you need to know first to understand office politics is that each organization has a unique culture. All organizations have developed certain method of behaviors that are unknown completely until you are a part of the organization. You must take the time when entering an organization to listen, observe, and learn the culture. Identify the authoritative figures within the organization and discover their expectations. Is it the culture one of micromanagement or is it unstructured? *The most important question is whether or not you fit the culture of the company*. Cultural fit is where most people get confused and fail to realize why they are not happy at their current place of employment. If you are in a company that demands breaks be taken at a certain time and you strongly believe in flexibility, the environment may not be a good fit for you; you will be unhappy. Many people complain about how their organization functions, but are not willing to change their circumstances; which stems from a lack of self-understanding and understanding of the organization.

TO ENGAGE IN
OFFICE POLITICS,
YOU HAVE TO
UNDERSTAND THE
DYNAMICS. BE AWARE
OF OTHERS'
INTERACTIONS AND
HOW YOUR BEHAVIOR
IS VIEWED

MICHELLE PENELOPE

GET RID OF THE BAD APPLES

What are things in your life with which you are not happy? The issues could be people or your actions. It will be important for you to analyze this question and be 100% honest with yourself. Your lack of satisfaction in any one area will have a significant impact on your productivity at work. People show their unhappiness in different ways. Based on the number of hours spent at work, many opportunities exist for things to occur that will make you unhappy, which could occur without you knowing it. To avoid this situation, create relationships and habits that give you peace. You will always encounter people or things you do not like. Control what you can in life and avoid things you do not like. If there are habits and people you can afford to eliminate, quickly take action. If you are not happy with your job and have made every attempt to make it better, and it still does not change, move on. If there are people at work who annoy you and you cannot get away from them, minimize your interactions with them as much as possible. If the person is your boss, read the section of knowing your boss and reassess the interactions. If you have tried everything to be happy and nothing   works, it may be a clear sign that you need to begin looking for another job.

SURROUND YOURSELF
WITH POSITIVITY.
LEARN FROM THE
NEGATIVE BUT FOCUS
ON THE POSITIVE

DR. ERIC ROBERTS

ADAPT TO YOUR BOSS

Getting to know your boss is one of the most important aspects of job satisfaction. However, knowing your boss does not mean you have to know him or her on a personal level. In fact, you do not have to like your boss to adapt to his or her style of leadership. The goal is to **know your boss's agenda**. What areas does your boss focus on? What are your boss's professional goals? What motivates your boss? If you know the answer to such questions, you will have a good chance of having an easier time in your job.

Every boss will be different. All of bosses are motivated by something. When people are in management roles, they tend to deal with multiple stressful situations. There is always a reason why they are willing to endure the stress. Regardless of whether they are motivated by their salary or personal satisfaction, you want to be the employee who supports and protects their agenda. Minimize your boss's stress. You can accomplish this by creating a positive work environment or taking on additional responsibilities. Once you know your boss's likes and dislikes, carefully manage your behaviors accordingly. Find a way to have your daily routines be supportive and not a hindrance to your boss.

All of your routines will change according to each one of your bosses. They will all be different and you must be willing and able to adapt.

DO NOT CREATE PROBLEMS FOR YOUR BOSS BUT CREATE SOLUTIONS TO YOUR BOSS' S PROBLEMS

INV. MENDEZ

HAVE GOOD TIME MANAGEMENT SKILLS

There are many different goals and ideas you will have throughout your lifetime. It is critical to be selective regarding goals and ideas. Choose them carefully, because you may not have time to complete them all. Using your time effectively is one of the most important skills in life. Most people fail to be efficient with their actions, using time unproductively. ***The ultimate use of your time occurs when your current actions are setting you up for future success.*** If all of your decisions are based on resolving current issues, then you are not using your time wisely. Do not let things fall behind. Take the necessary actions now that will allow you to complete tasks prior to their due dates. There is no better feeling than to be done with a task before its deadline. Meeting deadlines in advance must become routine for you if you are to be successful and at peace with your daily routine.

UNTIL WE MANAGE TIME, WE CAN MANAGE NOTHING ELSE

PETER DRUCKER

HAVE GREAT WORK ETHIC

Work ethic is the ability to do whatever it takes to get the job done. You must be willing to spend the time and energy necessary to achieve the desired goal. Most people do not work hard enough to get desired results. Never look to do the least amount of work possible. Do not avoid hard or challenging tasks. There will never be a convenient time to accept a challenge. Enjoy the experience of trying something new, because this will allow you to grow personally and professionally.

More than your words, your actions will define who you are as a person. What you do will always be a good indication of who you are as a person. The only way to be successful is to work as hard as possible. Most people do not know the amount of work it takes to achieve the success they desire. They want the maximum results while doing the least amount of work. This is not you. Do not compare yourself with others. You may work harder than everyone else and still not receive additional praise or income. Do not work hard because you want others to recognize you, but work hard because this is who you are. Learn to enjoy working hard, which is why you are reading this book.

OPPORTUNITIES ARE USUALLY DISGUISED AS HARD WORK, SO MOST PEOPLE DO NOT RECOGNIZE THEM

ANN LANDERS

BENEFIT FROM FAILURE

Do not be afraid to fail or make mistakes. It is okay to fail. Make sure you analyze the circumstances carefully that led to the failure and make the necessary adjustment to ensure that failure will not happen again. Individuals who avoid situations where they may fail will never achieve success. Always seek to do your best and know that you have done everything possible to succeed. Avoid being disappointed in yourself or comparing yourself to others. We are all different and will obtain different results. ***When you fail or do not accomplish your goal, embrace it as an opportunity*** to learn more about yourself and then move on. If you are open and honest with yourself about why you did not achieve success, you will begin to learn more about yourself. As a result, you will evolve and mature, which allows you to avoid making the same mistakes again.

You may encounter a situation where your failure is a result of another person's actions. Do your best not to put yourself in this type of situation. If there is no other option and this happens, learn from the situation. Analyze how you ended up in that particular situation and look for the signs that may have indicated the poor outcome was going to occur. Never hold a grudge against anyone; however, you may want to discuss the outcomes with the others involved. The failure has already happened; therefore you must be willing to learn and continue to look towards a more positive future.

THERE ARE NO
SECRETS TO
SUCCESS. IT IS THE
RESULT OF
PREPARATION, HARD
WORK, AND LEARNING
FROM FAILURE

COLIN POWELL

HAVE GOOD WORK LIFE BALANCE

This topic is one of the most important areas for you to understand. The relationship between your personal life and your professional life will have a major impact on your success in either or both areas. Let me be very clear when I say, *you must always take time to focus on your personal growth*. If you want professional growth, you will be expected to spend more time working than the average person. This is okay, but you will also have to disconnect at some point. If you have a family, make sure to value the time spent with them. It is important to discuss with individuals in your personal life the amount of time you need to spend at work. Discussions and open communication will allow them to realize you are not intentionally neglecting them, but only want to make sure you are doing a good job.

It is very important to understand that your job is how you will survive and pay your bills, but your personal and home life will be your legacy. The time spent outside of work will be how you will be remembered. Unless you are the owner of the organization, the time you spend at work can be eliminated by someone else's poor decisions. You must never sacrifice your personal growth for something that another person can take away. Having balance is very important. Always be willing to work hard and invest the necessary time to be successful, but never forget about yourself or your loved ones.

YOU CAN' T DO A GOOD JOB IF YOUR JOB IS ALL YOU DO

UNKNOWN

You are now prepared to be Happier At Work!

ABOUT THE AUTHORS

Dr. Eric Roberts is a leader in the field of Education who received his Ph.D in Educational Leadership and has held management roles for over a decade. He is an Alumni of the United States Naval Academy, Annapolis, Maryland. His knowledge of leadership and management stem from his years as a college football player, Naval Officer and management roles in Academia. Dr. Roberts' experience in both the military and civilian sectors give him a unique perspective of the workforce. He has held Academics positions such Director and Dean of Academic Affairs. Dr. Roberts' mission is to share his knowledge with others in an effort to help them achieve their goals.

Investigator Lorena Mendez was born in Montevideo, Uruguay and immigrated to the United States in 2000. She has many years of experience in communication. Investigator Mendez held Management positions in the areas of Retail, Customer Service, Food Service Industry and Education. She obtained a degree in Criminal Justice and a degree in Crime Scene Investigation. Inv. Mendez attended the Police Academy initiating her career in Criminal Justice as a Police Officer and gaining practical experience in the field of Investigation. She decided to work for the private sector and became a Field Investigator pursing her passion for interviewing and learning from a wide variety of personalities and cultures. Inv. Mendez focuses on the art of Management, regardless the field of work but specializes in interpersonal relationships.

LIFE IS SHORT

BE HAPPY

www.ingramcontent.com/pod-product-compliance
Lightning Source LLC
Chambersburg PA
CBHW050955050426
42337CB00051B/1255